Matthew 15-28

KENNETH O. GANGEL

VICTOR BOOKS®

A DIVISION OF SCRIPTURE PRESS PUBLICATIONS INC.
USA CANADA ENGLAND

Recommended Dewey Decimal Classification: 226.2
Suggested Subject Heading: BIBLE, N.T.—MATTHEW

Library of Congress Catalog Card Number: 88-60215
ISBN: 0-89693-460-8

VICTOR BOOKS
A division of SP Publications, Inc.
          Wheaton, Illinois 60187

CONTENTS

How to Use This Study

Personal Growth Bible Studies are designed to help you understand God's Word and how it applies to everyday life. To complete the studies in this book, you will need to use a Bible. A good modern translation of the Bible, such as the *New International Version* or the *New American Standard Bible*, will give you the most help. (NOTE: the questions in this book are based on the *New International Version.*)

You will find it helpful to follow a similar sequence with each study. First, read the introductory paragraphs. This material helps set the tone and lay the groundwork for the passage to be studied. Once you have completed this part of the study, spend time reading the assigned passage in your Bible. This will give you a general feel for the contents of the passage.

Having completed the preliminaries, you are then ready to dig deeper into the Scripture passage. Each study is divided into several sections so that you can take a close-up look at the smaller parts of the larger passage. These sections each begin with a synopsis of the Scripture to be studied in that section. Following each synopsis is a two-part study section made up of *Explaining the Text* and *Examining the Text*.

Explaining the Text gives background notes and commentary to help you understand points in the text that may not be readily apparent. After reading any comments that appear in *Explaining the Text*, answer each question under *Examining the Text.*

At the end of each study is a section called *Experiencing the Text.* The questions in this section focus on the application of biblical principles to life. You may find that some of the questions can be answered immediately; others will require that you spend more time reflecting on the passages you have just studied.

The distinctive format of the Personal Growth Bible Studies makes them easy to use individually as well as for group study. If the majority of those in your group answer the questions before the group meeting, spend most of your time together discussing the *Experiencing* questions.

If, on the other hand, members have not answered the questions ahead of time and you have adequate time in your group meeting, work through all of the questions together.

However you use this series of studies, our prayer is that you will understand the Bible as never before, and that because of this understanding, you will experience a rich and dynamic Christian life. If questions of interpretation arise in the course of this study, we recommend you refer to the two-volume set, *The Bible Knowledge Commentary*, edited by John F. Walvoord and Roy B. Zuck (Victor Books, 1984, 1986).

Introduction to the Gospel of Matthew

Matthew Levi was a publican who became one of the 12 disciples and after serving the Lord throughout the time of the Gospels, disappeared from church history after Acts 1:13. His name means "gift of God" and in His grace God recognized that gift by allowing this humble servant to write the first book of the New Testament.

The first half of Matthew stresses the life and ministry of Jesus Christ, the messianic King of the Jews. Matthew geared his arguments and historical record to present the Gospel of the Jewish King to any who were familiar with the prophecies of the Messiah. He intended to prove that Jesus of Nazareth was that Christ and to explain to any Gentile who might read his book the way in which the Old Testament was fulfilled in Christ.

Since he wrote primarily to Jews, however, this Gospel gives more place than any of the other three to the didactic (teaching) ministry of Christ. In fact, some 60 percent of the Gospel deals with the discourses of our Lord. Only in this Gospel is the word *church* found, but the key words are *king* and *kingdom.*

Nine well-known records of the life of Christ are peculiar to Matthew including such familiar themes as the wise men, the parable of the 10 virgins, and the suicide of Judas. Obviously these particular accounts were special to Matthew's purpose to convince Jews that Jesus the Messiah was their King.

Like the Book of Genesis in the Old Testament, Matthew forms a foundation for our understanding of the New Testament, particularly the movement from presenting the Gospel of the King to Jews only, toward the universal appeal proclaimed by Paul and other members of the missionary team.

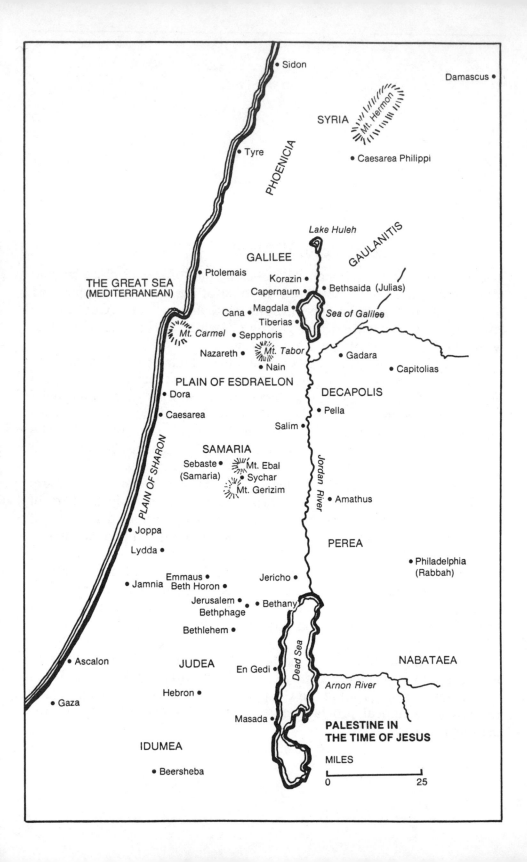

Sidon

Damascus

SYRIA

Mt. Hermon

Caesarea Philippi

Tyre

PHOENICIA

Lake Huleh

GALILEE   GAULANITIS

THE GREAT SEA
(MEDITERRANEAN)

Ptolemais

Korazin

Capernaum   Bethsaida (Julias)

Cana   Magdala   Sea of Galilee

Tiberias

Mt. Carmel   Sepphoris

Nazareth   Mt. Tabor

Nain   Gadara

Capitolias

PLAIN OF ESDRAELON   DECAPOLIS

Dora   Pella

Caesarea

Salim

SAMARIA

Sebaste   Mt. Ebal
(Samaria)   Sychar
Mt. Gerizim

Amathus

Joppa

Lydda   PEREA

Philadelphia
(Rabbah)

Emmaus   Jericho
Jamnia   Beth Horon

Jerusalem   Bethany
Bethphage

Bethlehem

Ascalon   JUDEA   En Gedi

Arnon River

NABATAEA

Gaza

Hebron

Masada

**PALESTINE IN
THE TIME OF JESUS**

IDUMEA

MILES

Beersheba

0   25

Plain of Sharon

Jordan River

Dead Sea

Matthew 15:1-39

Ministry of the King

Recently my wife and I completed a six-part teaching video series to accompany our newest book on the Christian home, *Building a Christian Family*. We used a number of vignettes in the video series including a segment of three elementary school teachers discussing how children reflect the values and behaviors of their families in the classroom. Two of the three teachers were kindergarten teachers who affirmed they could tell a great deal about the homelife of almost any child simply by watching the way that child behaved at school.

So it is with the wider relationship of family and society. A society consists of families. Mutual interaction between the wider society (culture) and the families in that culture is a topic of never-ending study for anthropologists as well as a source of great concern for God's people, who must live in this world as it is.

From the beginning of His ministry, Jesus made it clear that His people were to be in the world but not of it. He lived in that pattern and the disciples, following in His footsteps, did the same. Foremost in His teaching was the fact that believers are pilgrims and strangers in an alien society. No help should be anticipated; no affirmation would be forthcoming. The world is the enemy of the Father, the Son, and the children.

Such was the world in which Jesus ministered in the first century. Matthew 15 shows the unbelief of the Pharisees, the faith of the Canaanite woman, and the amazing feeding of the 4,000. You may find it helpful to read Mark 7:1–8:9 to get a different viewpoint on these incidents since Mark's account runs parallel with Matthew's chapter. Notice throughout the chapter how our Lord is a model of ministry for His disciples in the immediate sense and for all of us in the fuller sense. What a joy to study the ministry of the King.

A. THE MINISTRY OF REBUKE (*Matt. 15:1-9*). "Tradition!" sings Tevye in "Fiddler on the Roof" when asked to explain all the strange traditions of his Jewish people living in the little Russian town of Anatevka. The attitudes of the Pharisees in the first century were essentially the same. Whenever confronted by something or someone different from the sacred system they espoused, they complained about the breaking of tradition. This first portion of chapter 15 deals with the King's answer to the problem of tradition.

Examining the Text	*Explaining the Text*
1. Read Matthew 15:1-9. Do you think the Pharisees and teachers were sincere when they asked Jesus about breaking traditions?	
2. Why didn't Jesus' disciples engage in washing rituals?	2. The reference to "washing" in verse 2 dealt with more than just a simple washing of the hands—it spoke of a ceremonial ritual (Mark 7:1-5).
3. What could a Jew say to be relieved of providing parental support? What did this statement mean?	3. Our Lord points out the Pharisees' contempt for the Old Testament by the way they handled parental support. This situation was tantamount to income tax evasion today but here the priests made the profit (Mark 7:6-13).
4. How do verses 8-9 (Isa. 29:13) fit the rebuke?	

Explaining the Text	*Examining the Text*
	5. How do you feel when certain traditions in your church are changed?

B. THE MINISTRY OF TEACHING (*Matt. 15:10-20*). The last phrase of the previous section leads into this important passage on Jesus' teaching. He had just quoted from Isaiah about false teaching consisting only of rules taught by men (v. 9). Now the true Teacher offers the striking contrast. The Pharisees were blind leaders of the blind, plants not planted by God the Father, ultimately destined to spiritual failure for themselves and all who followed them. John F. Walvoord wrote: "Occupation with the outward religious ceremony, instead of inner transformation of the heart, has all too often attended all forms of religion and has plagued the church as well as it has Judaism" (*Matthew: Thy Kingdom Come*, Moody Press). The true Teacher emphasizes the inner life rather than that external ceremony.

Explaining the Text	*Examining the Text*
1. God had given the Jews the Law as a good tool to guide them to His truth. Now the radical teaching of the Messiah points out how the Law was misused.	1. Read Matthew 15:10-20. Why was the Pharisees' dependence upon tradition so dangerous?
	2. Why is the blindness analogy appropriate in this situation?

Examining the Text	Explaining the Text
3. Reword verse 18 in modern language as you would teach it to a small child.	
4. Write seven substitute words for the evil things that can come "out of the heart" (v. 19).	4. Verses 16-20 are an enlargement on Jesus' previous statement in Matthew 15:11.
5. What is the most important thing for a person to do who is truly concerned about being "clean"?	

C. THE MINISTRY OF HEALING (*Matt. 15:21-28*). Geographically, Jesus now moved to the northwest coast near the site of Tyre and Sidon. There He encountered a Syrophoenician woman (Mark 7:24-30) who demonstrated more faith than He had seen among the Jews in Israel. These verses demonstrate the power of prevailing prayer based on simple but genuine faith.

Examining the Text	Explaining the Text
1. Read Matthew 15:21-28. Using the map on page 9, locate Tyre and Sidon so you can identify exactly where Jesus went on this trip.	1. Tyre was located 35 miles from Galilee, and Sidon another 25 miles north. These cities were prominent in the Gentile coastline where centuries earlier the area's inhabitants were called "Canaanites" (Num. 13:29).

Explaining the Text

2. The Canaanite woman endured three rebuffs—silence (v. 23), rejection (v. 24), and insult (v. 26). Yet she was humble enough to take the title of "dog" if it meant Jesus would extend some blessings to her in her need.

Examining the Text

2. How do you feel about Jesus' first response to the woman? Why did He seemingly speak so harshly?

3. What seems to be the woman's perception of Jesus' identity?

4. List two or three points of contrast between this woman and the Pharisees.

5. What is the most important lesson you learned from this record of the Canaanite woman?

D. THE MINISTRY OF CARING (*Matt. 15:29-39*). As in the feeding of the 5,000 earlier, Jesus involved the disciples in the actual discussion of the crowd's hunger as well as allowing them to distribute the food. This portion of study begins with Jesus' return to Galilee from the northwestern coast and ends with a trip down to an area just north of Tiberias on the west shore of the Sea of Galilee.

Examining the Text

1. Read Matthew 15:29-39. Describe two or three results of the miracles described in verses 29-31.

Explaining the Text

2. Read about the feeding of the 5,000 in Matthew 14:13-21. Write at least three differences between the feeding of the 5,000 (14:13-21) and the feeding of the 4,000 in this passage. You may want to look ahead at Matthew 16:9-10.

2. Matthew recorded the feeding of the 4,000 in addition to the feeding of the 5,000 because he probably wanted to show that Jesus healed both Jews and Gentiles; fed both Jews and Gentiles; and ministered to "clean and unclean."

3. What did the disciples learn from the feeding of the 5,000?

3. The word for *basket* in verse 37 is *spuridas*, quite different from the word *kophinous* in 14:20. The latter refers to a small basket while the other is much larger.

4. Suggest three things Jesus' activities in these verses tell us about His love and compassion for people.

Experiencing the Text

1. Name two or three rituals you or your church currently observe. Do they have a basis in Scripture?

2. In what ways does Isaiah 29:13 apply today?

3. What substitute word would you use today for "unclean"?

4. How has the "produce" of your mouth changed since you've become a Christian?

5. When Jesus healed Gentiles, He broke tradition. Can you think of any ways in which you break tradition to serve Christ today?

6. Name some specific ways you can demonstrate caring in your family, church, and community.

Matthew 16:1-20

Mandate of the King

Every time a popular politician wins an election at the local, state, or national level, we hear that the people have given him "a mandate" to carry out his platform and set into motion reforms promised during his campaign. Though Jesus the Messiah was not elected, He was appointed by a Sovereign God and sent to earth as our Saviour with a clear-cut mandate.

Throughout the early years of His ministry Jesus said very little to His disciples or anyone else about the mandate He had been given by His Father. Almost everyone—Pharisees, Sadducees, crowds, disciples—misunderstood why He had come. Speculation grew with every miracle. Opposition built with every parable. The most earnest and devout individuals pondered the mysterious yet obviously supernatural character of Jesus' works.

Someone has said that the modern church needs to learn more about the "great commitment" before it can understand the "Great Commission." We talk a great deal about world evangelization and a global Gospel, yet churches fail to meet their budgets, programs are dropped for lack of funding, and the mission fields continue to cry for people with genuine commitment. Perhaps once again we need to understand the magnificence of Jesus' mandate.

A. PORTRAIT OF THE MANDATE (*Matt. 16:1-4*). Compare these verses with Matthew 12:38-42. The Lord continually refers to Jonah, stamping that prophet's experience as typology. Note too that the Pharisees and Sadducees, theological enemies in normal times, were united through their hatred for the truth.

Explaining the Text	Examining the Text
1. As far as we know, this is the first time the Pharisees and Sadducees were in agreement during the ministry of Jesus.	1. What do you think motivated the Pharisees and Sadducees to "test" Jesus?
2. The Pharisees were very religious, but spiritually they were in the same state as the Ninevites to whom Jonah preached.	2. Read Matthew 12:40. What is the "sign of Jonah"?
	3. Are people still looking for miraculous signs today?
	4. What should Christians today be doing to "interpret the signs of the times"?
	5. For what reasons did Jesus refer to the people of His day as an "adulterous generation"?

B. PERCEPTION OF THE MANDATE (*Matt. 16:5-12*). In this passage, the feeding of the 4,000 and 5,000 served as a lesson for the disciples. In Scripture, leaven almost always symbolizes permeating evil. Jesus wanted the disciples to understand His mandate which required recognizing the evil thinking of the Pharisees and Sadducees.

Examining the Text	*Explaining the Text*
1. Read Matthew 16:5-12. Why did Jesus use yeast to illustrate and describe the teaching of the Pharisees and Sadducees? Look ahead to Matthew's explanation in verse 13.	
2. In what ways can Christians be "careful" and "on guard"? (vv. 5-7)	
3. Did Jesus intend to scold the disciples with His questions? Or was He merely explaining Himself?	3. This is the fourth time in Matthew's Gospel that Jesus used the phrase "little faith" (6:30; 8:26; 14:31).
4. How do you think the disciples felt about their lack of understanding?	
5. Using a Bible dictionary, research the teachings of the Pharisees and the Sadducees. State three or four ways their teachings differed from each other.	5. Though their differences were many, the Pharisees essentially stood for tradition and the Sadducees for rationalism or an antisupernatural religion.

C. PERSON OF THE MANDATE *(Matt. 16:13-16)*. Coming to the borders of Caesarea Philippi, Jesus asked His disciples serious questions about their faith in Him (Mark 8:27-30; Luke 9:18-21). It may be important to note that Matthew alone records the expression, "of the living God."

Explaining the Text

1. The phrase "Son of man" has its roots in Ezekiel 2:1 and Daniel 7:13-14. Jesus emphasized humanity in order to lead the disciples to a confession of deity.

Examining the Text

1. Read Matthew 16:13-16. Why did some people think Jesus was John the Baptist or Elijah or Jeremiah?

2. What answers might people give today if asked the question of verse 15? How would you answer the question Jesus asked His disciples?

3. The word *Christos* is the New Testament equivalent of the Old Testament word *Messiah* which means "the anointed one." When Jesus acknowledged that He was the Messiah, He was acknowledging that He was God.

3. What three significant theological truths can be found in Peter's answer? (v. 16)

4. What did Jesus mean by "the gates of Hades"? In what ways does the church triumph over this evil force?

Examining the Text

5. Consider the entire context of Matthew 16. What did Jesus mean by "the keys of the kingdom of heaven"? For further information, examine Luke 11:52 and Revelation 1:18; 3:7; 9:1.

Explaining the Text

D. PEOPLE OF THE MANDATE (*Matt. 16:17-20*). Matthew recorded in these verses something that other Gospel writers did not include—Jesus' prophecy regarding the foundation of the church. The church was not built on Peter but on the One to whom Peter had attributed a special relationship with God.

Examining the Text

1. Read Matthew 16:17-20. Why does verse 17 suggest Peter was blessed?

2. What did Jesus mean when He said that "the gates of Hades" will not overcome His work of building the church?

3. Why did Jesus want His disciples not to tell anyone that He was the Christ?

Explaining the Text

1. Peter's answer came not from the traditionalism of the Pharisees nor the rationalism of the Sadducees, but rather a revelation of God through the Holy Spirit.

2. The word *church* in verse 18 refers to the universal body of believers, not to any particular local congregation or denomination.

3. Most evangelical commentators agree that "keys" refers to the authority found in the message of the Gospel.

Explaining the Text	Examining the Text
	4. How do you think Simon felt about having his name changed? Briefly explain the significance of the name change.

Experiencing the Text

1. How physical is your faith? On a scale of A through F (with F meaning greatest need), grade your need for "signs" to trust God on important matters in your life.

2. How would you live differently if you knew Jesus were coming next week? Next year?

3. Notice the future-tense verbs used by Jesus in verses 18-19. What are some specific ways Jesus is building His church today? How are you personally involved in His building program?

Matthew 16:21–17:13

Majesty of the King

In the fall of 1987, the President of the United States went to war with Congress over the nomination of Robert Bork as a Justice of the Supreme Court. Perhaps you remember how the charges were hurled back and forth, charges about the "imperial presidency" and "imperial congress." Somehow, say some Americans, we simply can't wean ourselves away from the monarchial systems in Europe which gave birth to American colonialism over 200 years ago.

It may very well be more difficult for people in a representative republic to grasp the concept of monarchy. We think the behavior of the British somewhat strange as they bow and revere their queens and princes. Yet that relationship much more closely approaches the link between King Jesus and His people. The New Testament unfolds slowly, revealing the majesty of the Heavenly Monarch.

This idea of imperialism and majesty are very much a part of this study in Matthew. Matthew introduces the imperial Saviour, the imperial Messiah who comes from the Father as His authoritative representative on earth. Small wonder Christians rejoice in singing Jack Hayford's chorus:

Majesty

Majesty, worship His majesty.
Unto Jesus be all glory, honor, and praise.
Majesty, kingdom authority,
Flow from His throne unto His own;
His anthem raise.
So exalt, lift up on high the name of Jesus.
Magnify, come glorify Christ Jesus the King.
Majesty, worship His majesty.
Jesus who died, now glorified,
King of all Kings.

A. MAJESTY OF ATONEMENT (*Matt. 16:21-23*). Peter's concept of a conquering king led him to rebuke the Messiah—and get rebuked in return. The passage ends with the familiar yet poignant paragraph on discipleship.

Explaining the Text

1. Some have wondered why Jesus didn't make His death and Resurrection a central theme in His preaching right from the beginning. Since He offered Himself as King of the Jews, that offer could only have been genuine if it started out allowing the Jewish nation to respond precisely to that opportunity.

2. Notice how the disciples themselves were not ready to accept the Crucifixion. Their concept of the conquering Messiah had completely missed the suffering servant message of Isaiah and Jeremiah.

Examining the Text

1. Read Matthew 16:21-23. Use a Bible dictionary to identify the differences between elders, chief priests, and teachers of the Law (v. 21).

2. What was actually wrong with Peter's response in verse 22?

3. Explain Jesus' words, "You do not have in mind the things of God, but the things of men" (v. 23).

4. Have you ever said, "Never, Lord"? Can you recall the last time—and the results?

Examining the Text	*Explaining the Text*
5. How do you think Peter felt about Jesus' rebuke?	

B. MAJESTY OF DISCIPLESHIP (*Matt. 16:24-28*). This brilliant passage on the subject of discipleship also appears in Mark 8:34-38 and Luke 9:23-27. Someone has said, "The way up is down in the Christian life." Only by losing one's life can one save it; only by denying oneself can one achieve the glory of Christ

Examining the Text	*Explaining the Text*
1. Read Matthew 16:24-28. What does it mean to "take up one's cross"?	1. Note the contrast in this passage. The world offers immediate gain with ultimate loss; Christ offers immediate loss with ultimate gain.
2. What kinds of questions appear in verse 26, and why do you think Jesus uses them here?	2. This chapter clarifies the time element between the first (suffering) and second (glorious) advents of Christ. In verse 21 Jesus described the Crucifixion and Resurrection; in verses 24-26 He portrays the life of His followers between the advents; and in verse 27 He promises that He will come in His Father's glory
3. How do you interpret Matthew 16:28?	3. Jesus says that each person will be rewarded "according to what he has done" (v. 27). Apparently this applies equally to the saved and the lost

Explaining the Text	*Examining the Text*
	4. In one brief paragraph describe how the cross of Jesus Christ stays central in your life.
	5. What does Jesus choose as the primary motivation for discipleship?

C. MAJESTY OF KINGSHIP (*Matt. 17:1-9*). The drama on the Mount of Transfiguration starred Jesus with a supporting cast of Moses and Elijah as the highest representatives of the Old Testament. New Testament saints were represented by the inner circle of disciples—Peter, James, and John. The purpose of the Transfiguration seems to be a prophetic vision of what the future kingdom will be like, or, more particularly, what the King will be like.

Explaining the Text	*Examining the Text*
1. The Transfiguration experience showed the three disciples the real Son of God.	1. Read Matthew 17:1-9. Why did Jesus choose these three disciples over the rest? Would you have chosen the same support group?
2. Not only do Moses and Elijah represent great figures of the Old Testament, but they represent two major segments of the Old Testament—the Law and the Prophets.	2. Evaluate Peter's idea for the shelters (v. 4). What implication do you find in his suggestion?

Examining the Text	Explaining the Text
3. Why didn't Jesus want anyone to know what the disciples had witnessed?	3. The significance of the Transfiguration probably rests in the necessity for the disciples to experience a confirmation of the promises of the kingdom, the necessity of the Cross, the presence of Old Testament and New Testament saints in the kingdom, the reality of personality in the afterlife, and the tangible reality experience of eternal life!
4. Record all the emotions you think the disciples might have felt during their experience on the mountain.	
5. The Transfiguration experience was a dramatic moment in the life of the disciples, but it seems remote to the kinds of things we understand today. Name three or four important lessons from the Transfiguration account that you can integrate into your life today.	

D. MAJESTY OF PROPHECY (*Matt. 17:10-13*). Seeing Elijah on the mountain reminded the disciples of Malachi's prediction in Malachi 4:5-6. Jesus affirmed that "Elijah" had already come (in the form of John the Baptist), and the religious leaders of the nation did not recognize him.

Explaining the Text

1. Some believe the appearance of John as Elijah was only a partial fulfillment of Malachi's prophecies. But Jesus affirmed that everything necessary to bring in the messianic kingdom had been performed; only the rejection of the nation hindered that reality.

Examining the Text

1. Read Matthew 17:10-13. Then review Malachi 3:1, Matthew 11:14, and Luke 1:17. Write a brief paragraph on the role of John the Baptist as "Elijah."

2. What did Elijah, Jesus, and John the Baptist all have in common?

3. How did the disciples understand the ministry of John the Baptist prior to this conversation?

Experiencing the Text

1. Name some specific ways you have "lost your life" for Christ.

2. List the activities of your life designed to gain the world. Now make a second list of those activities designed to gain your eternal soul.

3. Name several things you can do to prepare for Jesus' coming.

Matthew 17:14–19:30

Mercy of the King

In preparation for the 1980 primary elections, several candidates of one of the major political parties held a general public discussion at Dartmouth College, airing their views on the issues of that campaign. One representative of a leading news magazine approached a young Dartmouth coed as she left the discussion and asked, "What did you think of the candidates?" Presumably, when asked that kind of question in that kind of setting, one should weigh the candidates and reflect on their relative stands regarding foreign affairs, human rights, and the economy. Ignoring all of these, the young lady responded by saying, "None of them seems to have any humility."

What a commentary on the attitudes of leaders in our day. And what a contrast to the example of the Lord Jesus. Christianity is countercultural or perhaps we could say, transcultural. Unbound by time or place, it makes its demands on every generation in every nation. One of those demands calls for gentleness and mercy. Those who name the name of Jesus and adhere to the Gospel need to demonstrate to the world the historic and ever present mercy of the King.

A. MERCY FOR SOCIETY (*Matt. 17:14-27*). Coming down from the mountain, the Lord was immediately confronted with grief and murmuring rather than glory and majesty. The description of the demon-possessed boy and the payment of the temple tax illustrate first that lack of faith, not the difficulty of healing, hinders the work of God. Though Christians are not primarily citizens of this world, they still have an obligation to respect the laws of civil government. Sandwiched between these two incidents is another announcement about the death and Resurrection of the Lord.

Examining the Text	Explaining the Text
1. Read Matthew 17:14-27. Why couldn't the disciples cast out the demon?	1. The phrase "nothing will be impossible" depends upon the will of God in any given situation. God is omnipotent, but the disciples would not always be asking and doing things within His will.
2. What in this passage caused the disciples to grieve?	2. The bare facts of the Cross are no longer hidden or spoken in riddles. Jesus specifically instructs His disciples in the reality and manner of the atonement.
3. How did Jesus "fulfill the law"?	3. Honesty and respect for government provide a pattern in New Testament Christianity (Rom. 13; 1 Peter 2).
4. What did Jesus mean by "faith that can move mountains"? (v. 20)	

Explaining the Text	*Examining the Text*
	5. Why did Jesus choose to pay taxes for Peter and Himself? Was there any significance in finding the coin in a fish's mouth?

B. MERCY FOR CHILDREN (*Matt. 18:1-14; 19:13-15*). Though these passages obviously represent different events in the ministry of Jesus, we can study them together because of their thematic similarity. When the disciples demonstrated their interest in the physical kingdom, Jesus again taught them of the spiritual kingdom. In His relationship with children, Jesus verbalized what He demonstrated in Matthew 15:21-28—that humility and lowliness are prerequisite for receiving God's grace.

Explaining the Text	*Examining the Text*
	1. Read Matthew 18:1-14 and 19:13-15. What qualities do children possess that Jesus also wants to see in adults?
	2. Name some ways people hinder children from coming to the Lord.
	3. What do you think Jesus meant by the strong language of 18:8-9?

Examining the Text	Explaining the Text
4. How does the parable of the sheep enhance the lesson Jesus was teaching? (18:10-14)	4. Matthew 18:10-14 is a beautiful but difficult passage to understand. One thing seems clear: God knows and watches over all children.
5. In 19:14, how do you understand Jesus' meaning of the phrase "the kingdom of heaven belongs to such as these"?	
6. Why did the disciples rebuke people who brought children to Israel?	
7. Jesus referred to "the things that cause people to sin" (18:7). What are some of those things?	

C. MERCY FOR OFFENDERS (*Matt. 18:15-35*). The proper method for settling differences among Christians in the church is found in this portion of Scripture. Personal handling must be tried first; if unresolved, then the church assembly must be involved. The emphasis on mercy takes parabolic form in the second half of the chapter when Jesus tells the story of the unmerciful servant.

Explaining the Text

1. Verse 18 seems to re-
fer to the collective authority of the church to discipline its own (Acts 5).

3. Peter's question in
verse 21 probably resulted
from Jesus' previous
teaching on discipline, but
the Lord quickly moved
the scene from collective to
personal forgiveness.

4. A denarius was a Ro-
man silver coin worth about
16 cents and represented
a laborer's daily wages.

Examining the Text

1. Read Matthew 18:15-35. How do you understand
the prayer promise found in verse 19? Are there any
limitations? Are there any exceptions?

2. Write a brief summary of the steps that should be
followed when disagreements occur between
believers.

3. What do you take to be the central lesson of this
passage?

4. Study carefully the parable of the unmerciful servant and rewrite it in a single paragraph placing the
story in a modern family setting. Identify each character—the king, the debtor, the fellow servant, the other
servants, and the jailers.

5. In what ways did Jesus' parable answer Peter's
question about forgiveness?

D. MERCY FOR THE DIVORCED (*Matt. 19:1-12*). The Pharisees' question in verse 3 probably hinged on their reaction to Jesus' words in 5:31-32 which contradicted Talmudic teaching on divorce. Some evangelicals suggest that this passage teaches one legitimate reason for divorce—marital unchastity. Others argue that there is no legitimate evidence for that position since they consider that the words *fornication* and *adultery* refer to different things.

Examining the Text	*Explaining the Text*
1. Read Matthew 19:1-12. What did the Pharisees want to gain by raising the question of divorce?	1. Notice when the question arose, Jesus appealed to the law of creation and linked marriage to the original creation plan of God.
2. How did Jesus answer the Pharisees' question about Moses' permission?	2. The word for marital unfaithfulness in our text is *porneia*. Whatever the word means in the context of divorce, it is certainly clear from this passage that Jesus affirmed the permanence of marriage.
3. Review Matthew 5:31-32, Romans 7:1-3, and 1 Corinthians 7:10-16. Then state your belief regarding divorce.	
4. Why did Jesus refer back to Creation? (vv. 4-5)	
5. How would the divorce rate in churches be affected if Christians really believed and practiced what Jesus was teaching in this passage?	

E. MERCY FOR THE WEALTHY (*Matt. 19:16-30*). These practical verses contrast the attitudes of affluence with the denial of discipleship. The rich young ruler was complimentary, but he was not a worshiper. His shallow trust in riches was immediately revealed by the questioning of Jesus. In contrast, Jesus taught the disciples to willingly surrender earthly possessions with a view toward the significance and eternality of heaven.

Explaining the Text

1. Unfortunately, the young man represents all religious lost people whose great possessions prevent them from coming to the One from whom they can receive saving grace.

2. The "eye of the needle" passage is a familiar text. Surely Jesus intends to say that just as it is impossible for a camel to go through the eye of a needle, so it is impossible for anyone to be saved apart from the grace of God.

Examining the Text

1. Read Matthew 19:16-30. What is the basic difference between the young man's values and those displayed by Jesus?

2. Explain your interpretation of verse 30.

3. What did Jesus mean when He said, "It is hard for a rich man to enter the kingdom of heaven"? (v. 23)

Experiencing the Text

1. How does your view of paying taxes compare with Jesus' perspective?

2. What are you doing in your home, church, and community to bring little children to Jesus?

3. Grade yourself on your record of forgiveness. Can you name any person(s) you need to forgive right now?

4. If you have been divorced, name one important lesson God taught you through that difficult experience

5. What have you given up to follow Jesus? How has He rewarded your sacrifice?

Matthew 20:1–21:22

Might of the King

Violent crime rose 45 percent between 1977 and 1986 while property crime increased 18 percent, according to data released by the Federal Bureau of Investigation. Information gathered from 16,000 police departments across the country deals with such categories as aggravated assault (up 15 percent); murder (up 9 percent); robbery (up 9 percent); burglary (up 5.5 percent); larceny, theft, and forcible rape.

The overall crime rate rose 7 percent in cities, 6 percent in suburban counties, and 4 percent in rural areas. Researchers have predicted crime levels will increase in the next decade as children of the baby boom generation reach the most crime-prone age-group, the late teens and early twenties.

Ever since Cain killed Abel, people have been trying to force their will on others through violence. But the word *might* in the title of this lesson does not refer to physical violence, but rather divine authority. One thing seems clear throughout the last chapters of the Gospel of Matthew— Jesus was in total control of everything that happened in His life.

The might and power of Jehovah reside in His Son. But the strength of the Lord's hand rested not in physical or military displays, but in the meekness of grace.

A. MIGHT OF SOVEREIGNTY (*Matt. 20:1-16*). The Parable of the Vineyard Workers teaches us that the principle of divine grace and sovereignty will be operative even in the giving of rewards. This parable immediately follows Jesus' teaching regarding the disciples' sacrifice.

Examining the Text

1. Read Matthew 20:1-16. What is the significance of each of the characters in this parable? Who is the landowner? Who were the hired men? What is the vineyard?

2. Do you think the workers who worked all day had a right to complain? How do you feel about the landowner's explanation?

3. What significance do you place on the fact that this parable immediately follows Jesus' description in 19:27-30 of how the disciples should minister?

4. In one sentence, summarize Jesus' teaching in this parable.

5. How does the idea of wages fit with a salvation given freely by God's grace?

Explaining the Text

1. The Parable of the Vineyard Workers answers Peter's question in 19:27 and appears only in the Gospel of Matthew.

3. The time slots identified in the parable are most likely 6:00 A.M., 9:00 A.M., 12:00 noon, 3:00 P.M., and 5:00 P.M. Remember the Jewish day always runs from 6:00 A.M. to 6:00 P.M.

4. Verses 13-15 seem complicated, but the singular emphasis points to the sovereignty of God.

Explaining the Text	Examining the Text
	6. Think of a time when you were envious of the Lord's generosity to others? How did He deal with you on that occasion?

B. MIGHT OF THE KINGDOM (*Matt. 20:17-34*). Sadly we find the disciples seeking prestige all too quickly after hearing the Parable of the Vineyard Workers. The general teaching of Jesus in this passage emphasizes that greatness in the church runs contrary to the world's concept of greatness. For the Christian, leadership becomes an attitude of service. Jesus demonstrated His own servant attitude by healing the blind men.

Explaining the Text	Examining the Text
1. Here is the first mention of crucifixion. The disciples were probably shocked and amazed at a prediction of the Roman form of execution.	1. Read Matthew 20:17-34. Notice how the announcement of the Crucifixion comes against the backdrop of verses 1-16. Why is that arrangement of the text so dramatic?
2. The two sons were later martyred; one very early in the record of the early church (Acts 12:1-2), and one, according to tradition, toward the end of the first century.	2. How do you account for the boldness of the mother of Zebedee's sons?
	3. In one word, what did Zebedee's sons want from Jesus?

Examining the Text	Explaining the Text
4. According to the text, what was the supreme example for the disciples demonstrating greatness through servanthood?	
5. Why did the crowd rebuke the blind men to be quiet?	

C. MIGHT OF THE KING (*Matt. 21:1-17*). The Triumphal Entry is sometimes celebrated with little concept of its meaning. The colt ridden by Jesus was part of prophetic necessity (Zech. 9:9) and the language with which the King was greeted comes from Psalm 118:6. The Messiah's first act in the city dramatically surprised the traditional Jews. Rather than overthrowing Rome He went to worship at the temple.

Examining the Text	Explaining the Text
1. Read Matthew 21:1-17. On a map, trace Jesus' route from Bethphage by the Mount of Olives to Jerusalem.	
2. Using a Bible dictionary, define the word *hosanna*.	2. Notice the explanation of Jesus' identity in verse 11. This refers to the promise of Moses in Deuteronomy 18:15 and appears in the questions of John the Baptist recorded in John 1.

Explaining the Text	Examining the Text
	3. Why were the chief priests and teachers of the law "indignant"? (v. 15)
	4. What do we learn about Christlike behavior from 21:1-5?
	5. Apart from the fulfillment of prophecy, what was the significance of the King of the Jews entering the city on a donkey?

D. MIGHT OF FAITH (*Matt. 21:18-22*). In the spring, the Palestinian fig tree puts out green figs with its leaves, guaranteeing the harvest. Symbolically the tree may stand for Israel as a nation, emphasizing the fact that Jesus, on entering the Holy City, found no "spiritual figs."

Explaining the Text	Examining the Text
1. Mark 11:12-14 makes it clear that the fig tree incident occurred on Monday morning and that the words of verses 21-22 occurred the next day (Mark 11:20-25). Such dating references are important in tracking the last week of Jesus' life and ministry.	1. Read Matthew 21:18-22. How do you account for Jesus' hunger? (v. 18)

Examining the Text

2. Why did Jesus deliberately destroy a part of His Father's creation?

3. How do you interpret the prayer promises in verses 21-22 in light of the overall New Testament teaching on prayer?

4. Notice the disciples' reactions to Jesus' action. Why were they amazed after all they had seen before?

Explaining the Text

2. The incident of the fig tree is essentially a lesson on faith and the miraculous power of God, though some see in it a typological reference to Israel.

Experiencing the Text

1. Name specific ways you work in God's kingdom today.

2. Compare Matthew 19:30 with Matthew 20:16. Is Jesus saying the same thing each time? What does it mean in your Christian life?

3. Note the clarity of the Gospel in 20:17-19. What can you do to make Christ's message clearer to people who don't understand it?

4. What ambitious goals do you have for yourself or your children? How have you taken God into account in each of them?

5. Name five specific ways you worship the Son of God.

6. If you had been there on the day of the Triumphal Entry, what would you have shouted?

7. Name some miracles you want God to do in your life and the life of your family.

8. How do you commonly respond to God's miracles in His world?

9. How can you genuinely activate Matthew 21:22?

Matthew 21:23–23:39

Mockery of the King

Short of the Crucifixion itself there is no more painful passage in Scripture than the description of how Jesus was beaten. He was repeatedly mocked by the crass and cruel scoffing of ignorant Roman soldiers.

But in chapters 21, 22, and 23, we see mocking of a different kind. Here sophisticated religious leaders twisted every word Jesus said, trying to find some way to trip Him up. Their mockery was subtle yet brutal as they denied the very truth Jesus brought to them, and, in so doing, condemned themselves and their nation.

Such behavior seems unfathomable to the modern mind. How could an entire nation fail to respond to God's gift of His own Son? How was it possible for many people to hear Jesus speak, see His miracles, and yet still laugh at His message?

Yet we recognize the control of the Father over every event on earth, even in a society darkened by the power of sin. And in this study we also recognize that not everyone rejected Him. The small remnant of believing Jews formed the nucleus of the New Testament church.

A. AUTHORITY OF THE KING (*Matt. 21:23-46*). In this passage, the Pharisees were left no recourse but verbal argument. Caught on the horns of a dilemma by Jesus' words, they knew Jesus told the Parable of the Two Sons and the Parable of the Tenants for them.

Explaining the Text	*Examining the Text*
1. The priests' references to "these things" in verse 23 probably refers to the excitement over the Triumphal Entry, the cleansing of the temple, and the most recent miracles.	1. Read Matthew 21:23-46. Why were the Pharisees so hesitant to render a judgment on the authority of John's baptism?
2. The Parable of the Two Sons explains that those who originally reject the Gospel and then are converted are better off than those who pay only lip service to the Lord.	2. What is the significance of each of the characters in the Parable of the Two Sons? In the Parable of the Tenants?
	3. Why do you think the tenants behaved so wickedly?
	4. Who is the capstone in verse 42? What did Jesus mean when He said some would be "broken to pieces" and others would be "crushed"? (v. 44)

Examining the Text	*Explaining the Text*
5. Who are the people to whom the kingdom of God will be given? (v. 43)	

B. WEDDING OF THE KING (*Matt. 22:1-14*). The king in this parable issued a gracious invitation, only to be rejected by those who would normally be expected to attend. A broad invitation was then extended to those unlikely to receive it. As a result, those actually chosen to attend were few.

Examining the Text	*Explaining the Text*
1. Read Matthew 22:1-14. Explain the symbolism of the king, the son, the servants, and the additional servants.	1. Some scholars suggest that the Parable of the Wedding Banquet depicts a general invitation of the Gospel which was rejected and then extended to the Gentiles. Others see in the parable an offer of the kingdom and a portrayal of the millennial age.
2. Why do you think the king said, "Those I invited did not deserve to come"? (v. 8)	2. British expositor G. Campbell Morgan sees three distinct invitations in this parable: the preaching ministry of Jesus; the general invitation of the early church to the nation of Israel; and the even more general message of the Gospel in which all are invited to come to the king, regardless of their background.
3. Why did the ill-dressed man receive such severe punishment?	

Explaining the Text	Examining the Text
	4. Describe how you would feel if you were invited to the king's wedding banquet.
	5. Which group in this account best reflects your response to the invitation?
	6. What did Jesus mean by His statement, "For many are invited but few are chosen"?

C. ISSUES BEFORE THE KING (*Matt. 22:15-46*). Three confrontations make up this portion of study. The first includes the Pharisees and the Herodians and focuses on taxes (Mark 12:13-17; Luke 20:20-26). The second pits Jesus against the Sadducees and deals with the illustration of marriage and the Resurrection (Mark 12:18-27; Luke 20:27-40). The third and final confrontation centers on the Pharisees and raises two questions: What is the greatest commandment? Whose Son is the Messiah?

Explaining the Text	Examining the Text
1. The question about Caesar's taxes is a reference to Tiberius Caesar who reigned from A.D. 14 to 37. However, the issue raises a question of allegiance to government in general rather than just to Tiberius Caesar.	1. Read Matthew 22:15-46. List three things that verses 15-21 teach us about Jesus.

Examining the Text

2. What was the Sadducees' primary mistake in the debate over marriage?

3. What does verse 30 suggest regarding marriage in heaven?

4. After studying this passage, how do you feel toward the Pharisees? The Herodians? The Sadducees? The crowd? Jesus?

5. In what ways is the Messiah the Son of David?

Explaining the Text

2. The Sadducees were the religious liberals of the first century whose theology had no room for resurrection, angels, or spirits (Acts 23:8). They attacked Jesus on a point at which His declaration of truth was very different from their belief system.

D. CONDEMNATION BY THE KING (*Matt. 23:1-39*). The hypocrisy of the Pharisees surely must have been obvious to all who knew them, but only John and Jesus called for public accountability. In the second section of the chapter (vv. 13-32), Jesus pronounced woes upon the Pharisees. Matthew alone records Jesus' scathing denunciation of the Jewish leaders. The chapter ends with the lament over Jerusalem, the heart of Jesus breaking over a people whom He loves and for whom He was about to die.

Explaining the Text	*Examining the Text*

Explaining the Text

1. A phylactery was a small leather pouch that contained strips of parchment with Old Testament verses. This pouch was usually tied to one's left arm and forehead.

Examining the Text

1. Read Matthew 23:1-39. Identify the sins of the Pharisees as found in verses 1-12.

2. Note the number of times the word *hypocrites* is used in this chapter.

3. Describe the change in Jesus' emotions between verses 33-36 and 37-39.

4. To what event do you think Jesus referred in verse 39?

Experiencing the Text

1. In what ways is Jesus' authority evident in your life? In the life of your family?

2. Think about how you came to Christ. How many times were you invited before you responded?

3. In what ways are you inviting "anyone you can find" to the King?

4. How can you implement Matthew 22:8-12 in your church?

5. Write out the seven woes using just one word for each woe. Now check those that apply to you or to your church.

6. Are there any topics in this chapter you would like your pastor to address in some future sermon? Why not write him a note and tell him about it?

Matthew 24:1-51

Mountain Teaching of the King—Part 1

Frequently we use the term "mountaintop experience" to describe a special encounter with God or the memorable moment in which we made a new commitment to Christ. Chapters 7 and 8 describe such a mountain-top experience enjoyed by the disciples on a day when Jesus taught them more about Himself. In the days following the Triumphal Entry, Jesus spent the daylight hours teaching in the temple and the evening hours instructing the disciples. One of these instruction periods took place outside the city on the Mount of Olives.

In their pride for the magnificent temple, the disciples pointed out its beauty to Christ. His startling response precipitated these questions: When will these things be? What will be the sign of Jesus' coming which will consummate the age?

Of these two questions, Matthew seems most concerned with the second which is logical in the light of what we know about His kingdom purposes. Luke records an expanded prophetic reference to the destruction of Jerusalem in A.D. 70 (Luke 21:12-24) whereas Matthew's account refers primarily to the end times.

In conjunction with the Old Testament, this teaching on the Mount of Olives is concerned with the seventieth week of Daniel's prophecy which takes place after the Rapture of the church (Dan. 9:20-27). This prophetic seventieth week is equated by many theologians with the seven years of Tribulation which will come upon the earth after the Lord takes His church home to be with Him (the Rapture).

Christians differ on when and how the Rapture will take place; some believe the entire church will be taken before the Tribulation; others that certain believers will be taken at the beginning and some later; "Midtribulationists" believe the church will pass through the first half of the Tribulation; and others contend that the church must pass through the entire Tribulation on earth. We should find it natural that Jesus wanted His disciples to grasp this teaching of the end times.

A. SIGNS OF THE END TIMES (*Matt. 24:1-8*). Central to this passage is Jesus' warning in verse 4. Verses 4-8 offer general characteristics of the age corresponding to Daniel's seventieth week. These signs have been partially fulfilled and should be recognized as the beginning rather than the end of the sorrows which mark the close of time.

Examining the Text	*Explaining the Text*
1. Read Matthew 24:1-8. Why did the disciples call Jesus' attention to the temple buildings?	1. Thinking historically, the disciples probably linked the destruction of the temple with the Captivity, remembering that sequence of events from 586 B.C.
2. Notice how many questions are found in verse 3.	2. Four disciples were involved in these initial questions—Peter, James, John, and Andrew.
3. List the signs of the times which appear in these verses.	3. The general signs of the times described in verses 4-8 correspond to some extent to the seven seals in Revelation 6.
4. What did Jesus say our response should be when we hear of war, famine, earthquakes, and other tragedies?	

B. PERSECUTION IN THE END TIMES (*Matt. 24:9-25*). Beginning in verse 9, the general signs of the previous five verses give way to a specific description of the Tribulation. They do not yet answer the direct question the disciples asked about the signs of the Lord's coming. Verses 15-25, however, point up the sign of the Great Tribulation, a fulfillment of Daniel's prophecy regarding "an abomination that causes desolation" (Dan. 9:27). Premillennial theologians refer to the last three and a half years of the seven-year Tribulation as the Great Tribulation.

Explaining the Text	*Examining the Text*
1. The persecution and apostasy described in verses 10-13 related to Jews in the Tribulation. Nevertheless, the conditions of spiritual salvation are not by works of endurance but rather by grace.	1. Read Matthew 24:9-25. Study Revelation 6–7 in connection with this section of our study.
	2. What did Jesus say the world's attitude toward His followers would be?
	3. In addition to the Daniel passages mentioned in the synopsis, study Matthew 24:15-25 in light of 2 Thessalonians 2:4 and Revelation 13:14-15.
4. Well-meaning people have been fooled for years by self-anointed date-setters who point to secret returns of Christ.	4. Name some "false Christs" alive during your lifetime. Identify some common themes of their preaching.

C. DESCRIPTION OF THE END TIMES (*Matt. 24:26-35*). The Second
Coming of Christ will be a public event, unlike the Rapture of the church. A
frightening display of divine disruption in the heavens will take place prior
to the Lord's coming to earth to bring in His earthly kingdom. The budding
of the fig tree offers a natural illustration used by Jesus to demonstrate His
imminent return. The buds are like signs and His coming like the summer.
The prophecy means certain fulfillment, but the day is unknown.

Examining the Text	*Explaining the Text*
1. Read Matthew 24:26-35. In what ways is lightning an appropriate simile for the Second Coming?	1. The strange phenomena accompanying the Second Coming were foretold as early as Isaiah 13:9-10 and Joel 3:15-16.
2. If the coming of the Lord is a happy time, why will an international mourning take place? (v. 30)	
3. To whom do the words "this generation" refer in verse 34?	
4. Rewrite verse 35 with a specific life-related ending. For example, "Heaven and earth will pass away, but God's promise to allow only temptations I can bear will never pass away."	4. Notice how the Lord inserts a warm promise after a frightening prophecy (v. 35).

Explaining the Text	Examining the Text
	5. What did Jesus mean by the phrase "Wherever there is a carcass, there the vultures will gather"? (v. 28)

D. WARNINGS ABOUT THE END TIMES (*Matt. 24:36-51*). To illustrate the Second Coming, Jesus referred to the historic flood in Noah's day. Like the Flood, the Second Coming will bring divine judgment to the earth as the Lord comes in power after the Tribulation to defeat His enemies and set up the millennial kingdom. Jesus emphasized the necessity of careful anticipation of His return much in the same way a good man keeps watch over his house since he doesn't know when a thief might come. These verses also call for service and preparation for the Lord's return. As Martin Luther once said, "I think the last day is not far away."

Explaining the Text	Examining the Text
	1. Read Matthew 24:36-51. How did Noah provide an apt model for the end times?
2. Severe persecution during the end days will cause true faithfulness to be rare. Temptation to deny the Lord and accept the mark of the beast will be strong. But the true and faithful servant will demonstrate his changed life by his endurance.	2. In a few words, identify the key message of verses 42-44.

Examining the Text	Explaining the Text
3. In verses 48-49, what mistake did the wicked servant make?	
4. What one thing can you say for sure about Jesus' return?	
5. Why doesn't God allow anyone to know the time of Christ's return?	

Experiencing the Text

1. In what specific ways are we helped or hindered in our worship by attractive buildings?

2. What troubles you most about the end of the world?

3. How can believers protect themselves from false teaching about the end times?

4. If you could ask God one question about the end times, what would it be?

5. What does it mean to "be ready" for the Lord's return?

6. On a scale of 1–10 (with 10 as excellent servanthood), how would you rate your servanthood in relation to the Lord's return?

Matthew 25:1-46

Mountain Teaching of the King—Part 2

The Olivet Discourse offers information found nowhere else in Scripture. In a very lengthy teaching segment, Jesus described the end of the age in colorful terminology and amazing detail. This is Matthew's final record providing information about the kingdom and the fulfillment of kingdom prophecies in the Old Testament.

To be sure, the disciples did not understand these prophecies. They failed to grasp the difference between postponement and annulment, and even after the death and Resurrection of the Lord, they asked questions about the coming of the kingdom (Acts 1:6).

Perhaps it is important for us when studying this passage to look beyond the controversy to life principles. Of course, we must understand the immediate meaning of the text and put it in proper interpretive perspective. But beyond that, the questions at the conclusion of our study give us fuel for Christian behavior *now*.

The following page contains a chart of the Olivet Discourse enabling us to put into perspective the various segments of Matthew 24–25 and to see how the Bible unfolds end-time events.

Chart of the Olivet Discourse

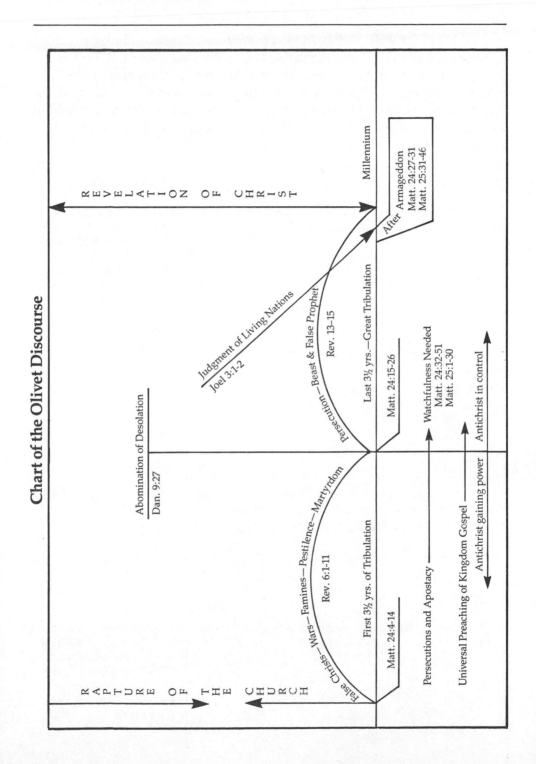

RAPTURE OF THE CHURCH

REVELATION OF CHRIST

False Christs—Wars—Famines—Pestilence—Martyrdom
Rev. 6:1-11

First 3½ yrs. of Tribulation
Matt. 24:4-14

Abomination of Desolation
Dan. 9:27

Judgment of Living Nations
Joel 3:1-2

Persecution—Beast & False Prophet
Rev. 13-15

Last 3½ yrs.—Great Tribulation
Matt. 24:15-26

Millennium

After Armageddon
Matt. 24:27-31
Matt. 25:31-46

Persecutions and Apostacy

Watchfulness Needed
Matt. 24:32-51
Matt. 25:1-30

Universal Preaching of Kingdom Gospel

Antichrist gaining power

Antichrist in control

A. PARABLE OF THE VIRGINS (*Matt. 25:1-13*). Common interpretations of this parable identify the virgins as the professing church, the oil as the symbol of the Holy Spirit, the cry at midnight as the preaching of the Second Coming, and the appearance of the bridegroom as the first (or only) return of Christ. But notice that Jesus mentions no bride throughout the parable and the context of the Olivet Discourse leads us not to a discussion of the church but rather a focus on Israel.

Examining the Text	*Explaining the Text*
1. Read Matthew 25:1-13. Identify ways that the virgins are similar. In what ways are they different?	1. Some have suggested the difference in the virgins refers to those who just *profess* salvation and those who genuinely *possess* it. In the Tribulation Israel may know when Jesus' coming is near because of the signs, but not all will be spiritually ready.
2. How would a wise person behave in relation to the Lord's return? A foolish person?	
3. Why did Jesus emphasize the unknown day and hour of His return since He had already dealt with this issue two or three times in this discourse?	
4. Describe the bridegroom's response to the foolish virgins.	4. A first-century Jewish wedding began at the home of the bride, later moving to the bridegroom's house for another phase of the ceremony including a marriage feast.

B. PARABLE OF THE TALENTS (*Matt. 25:14-30*). Like the previous parable, this one is often applied to the church. Talents are viewed as gifts which Christ has bestowed on believers. Verse 30 creates a problem for that view, however, when the unprofitable servant has to be condemned to judgment. In the context of the New Testament, we can accept neither a true believer who loses his salvation nor a professing believer on whom Christ bestowed spiritual gifts. Again, therefore, the best interpretation of the passage relates to Israel and the end times.

Explaining the Text	*Examining the Text*
1. You'll notice that in the realm of serving Christ the reward for a job well done is additional and increased responsibility!	1. Read Matthew 25:14-30. Identify the symbolic importance of each character in the parable—the man on a journey, the first servant, the second servant, and the third servant.
2. A silver talent could be worth as much as $2,000; a gold talent, up to $30,000. A normal daily wage in the first century was 16 cents; so these gifts represent an overwhelming amount.	2. Why did the man give different amounts of money to each servant?
3. The man who received one talent was deficient in works but he was condemned because of his lack of faith. The person who really believes the promises of Christ will believe the promise of His coming.	3. Write the main lesson of this parable.

C. PARABLE OF THE JUDGMENT (*Matt. 25:31-46*). This passage describes a period following the Second Coming. The Gentiles will be gathered before

Jesus, and the sheep and goats will be separated. The throne appears on earth, fulfilling the prediction of Jeremiah 23:5. The implication of these verses suggests that no Rapture of living saints occurs at the time of the Second Coming since that has already happened at the Rapture. Also, during the time between the Rapture and the revelation of Christ, a new body of saints made up of both Jews and Gentiles, has been created.

Examining the Text	*Explaining the Text*
1. Read Matthew 25:31-46. Why did Jesus use sheep and goats to describe the two kinds of people at the judgment?	1. Verse 31 takes us back to 24:30-31 as judgment was foretold in Joel 3:1-2.
2. In what ways can serving others be the same as serving Christ?	2. John Walvoord sees "these brothers of mine" (v. 40) as a third group of people different from both sheep and goats "which can only be identified as Israel, the only remaining people who are in contrast to all the Gentiles" (*Matthew: Thy Kingdom Come*, Moody Press, 1974, p. 201).
3. How do you interpret the "eternal punishment" mentioned in verse 46?	3. The basis of judgment in this passage seems to be a failure to extend mercy to Jewish believers during the Tribulation.
4. What phrases in this parable give us a clue that the sheep acted by faith and were not given eternal life on the basis of their good works?	

Explaining the Text	Examining the Text
	5. List the areas of service mentioned by Jesus in this passage.

Experiencing the Text

1. If oil represents the Holy Spirit, what steps can you take to make sure your lamp will not go out?

2. How should Christians "keep watch" for the coming of the Lord?

3. If the Master returned today, what would He have to say to you regarding the way you have used your talents?

4. How can the Parable of the Talents fit together with the Parable of the Sheep and the Goats to help us understand ministry for the Lord?

5. Review the three parables of Matthew 25. How do these three lessons apply in today?

Matthew 26:1-35

Mission of the King

One of the major rules of Bible study is the "principle of proportion." It suggests that God deliberately confers larger segments of Scripture to those events or teachings He wants to emphasize. Notice in Matthew that the last three chapters, more than 10 percent of the book, deal with the death and resurrection of Christ. In John, the principle is even more pronounced with chapters 12—21, nearly half the book, given over to the last week of His life.

It's important too that we understand the harmony of that last week; that is, to get things in proper order as the Gospels portray them. The chart on the following page shows six trials recorded in three of the four Gospels—three religious and three civil. Though none appear in this particular lesson, grasping the flow of events now will help us throughout the rest of our study in Matthew.

In addition to the evil plots of the chief priests and elders, Jesus faced betrayal and denial by His friends. In the midst of it all He repeatedly emphasized that everything that happened fit into God's plan as Jesus carried out the mission of the King.

Jesus' Six Trials

Religious Trials

Before Annas	John 18:12-14
Before Caiaphas	Matthew 26:57-68
Before the Sanhedrin	Matthew 27:1-2

Civil Trials

Before Pilate	John 18:28-38
Before Herod	Luke 23:6-12
Before Pilate	John 18:39–19:6

A. MISSION STATEMENT (*Matt. 26:1-5*). As we begin reading Matthew 26, only hours separate Jesus from Calvary's cross. Even as Jesus explains the Crucifixion to His disciples, the plot to kill Him is already underway.

Explaining the Text	*Examining the Text*
1. Despite the machinations of men, the King never surrendered control of His own destiny. For six months He had been pointing to the event and now He named the day.	1. Read Matthew 26:1-5. What was significant about the Son of man being crucified on the Passover?
	2. Did the disciples understand what was going to happen to Jesus?
3. The Passover was an important time in Jerusalem every year. Because of the large number of visitors and a general restlessness, the Roman governor always came down from Caesarea with additional troops during the week of Passover.	3. From your study in Matthew, what information would help you understand why Caiaphas seemed to hate Jesus so much?
4. It's important not to confuse the Passover with the Feast of Unleavened Bread. That would occur 10 days later when pilgrims would already have begun returning to their homes.	4. Why did the chief priests plan to arrest Jesus "in some sly way and kill him"? (v. 4)

B. MISSION SYMBOL (*Matt. 26:6-13*). Interesting, isn't it, that Matthew introduced the ominous account of the Crucifixion with a story of a dinner at Bethany honoring Jesus? But even this happy occasion pointed up the misunderstanding of the disciples, giving the Lord opportunity to teach them about motives.

Examining the Text	*Explaining the Text*
1. Read Matthew 26:6-13. Since lepers were unclean, what might we conclude about Jesus' decision to eat at Simon's house?	1. Matthew does not name the perfume, but both Mark and John say it was spikenard, a gift fit for a king. In fact, Heroditus lists it as one of five gifts sent by Cambyses to the King of Ethiopia.
2. Notice that several if not all of the disciples were indignant. What does this communicate about their understanding of the Gospel at this point?	2. John 12 tells us that Judas was the first to object, and he did so because he was motivated by personal gain.
3. Why did the woman choose to pour a jar of expensive perfume on Jesus' head?	3. The word for *waste* means ruin, destruction, or loss. These pragmatic disciples from poor backgrounds reacted quite normally to the woman's act, but in doing so, demonstrated their own failure to grasp what Jesus was saying.
4. Why did Jesus say that the woman's action in this passage would be remembered wherever the Gospel is preached?	

C. MISSION SUPPER (*Matt. 26:17-30*). The account of the Passover is recorded here as well as in Mark 14:17-21 and Luke 22:14-30. Luke adds the institution of the Lord's Supper, and John (13:1-12) records the incident of Christ washing the disciples' feet. None of the Gospel writers give details, and it appears Matthew provides only a concise summary. The important point in Matthew's summary is Judas' betrayal of Jesus, so he introduces that into the text almost immediately.

Explaining the Text

1. The chronology of events at the Last Supper probably followed this pattern: Jesus gave thanks before introducing the bitter herbs and serving the unleavened bread and the lamb. Then He ate the bitter herbs and the others did the same. Next Jesus mixed the wine and water. The group sang Psalms 113 and 114, and Jesus ceremonially washed his hands and broke the bread. Finally, the group joined Him in eating the food.

2. The word *reclining* (v. 20) refers to the custom of lying on couches arranged around the table low enough to eat from in that position.

Examining the Text

1. Read Matthew 26:17-30. Using a Bible dictionary or encyclopedia, write a paragraph summarizing the observation of the Feast of Passover.

2. Why did Judas refuse to admit his guilt in verse 25?

3. List some emotions the disciples may have felt during the Last Supper.

Examining the Text	*Explaining the Text*
4. What evidence is there that the disciples began to realize what was happening to their Master?	

D. MISSION SORROW (*Matt. 26:14-16; 31-35*). Two different portions of this passage describe unfaithful behavior by two different disciples. The first deals with Judas' betrayal, and the second, Peter's denial. As Jesus predicted the latter, He surely did so with deep sorrow, knowing what lay ahead that night

Examining the Text	*Explaining the Text*
1. Read Matthew 26:14-16; 31-35. Why did Judas initiate contact with the priests rather than their contacting him?	1. Thirty silver coins represented the redemption price paid for a slave (Ex. 21:32). The same amount was also prophesied by Zechariah as the price of the rejected Shepherd (Zech. 11:12)
2. What can we learn from this passage about Peter's level of understanding regarding the Resurrection?	
3. Were the disciples and Peter sincere when they said they would never disown Jesus? Why or why not?	

Experiencing the Text

1. Think back on events in your life. How has God's time schedule been evident?

2. How will people remember you? How do you want them to remember you?

3. Using Jesus' model, how can you find peace in times of crisis?

4. What hymn(s) would you choose for your own funeral?

5. Have you ever been betrayed or felt betrayed? What did you do about it?

Matthew 26:36-75

Misery of the King

According to the February 14, 1983 issue of *Newsweek* magazine, no accurate count is possible but some researchers estimate at least 10,000 political prisoners in the Soviet Union, perhaps 2,000 in Poland, as many as 15,000 in Turkey, and a minimum of 10,000 scattered across Africa. Nearly one half of the 157 members of the United Nations hold political prisoners of one kind or another.

In this passage, the Son of God became a political prisoner. In a mock trial before the Sanhedrin He was pronounced "worthy of death" and then sent to Pilate, the governor. In the next two lessons we will consistently find that the Jewish leaders on the authority of Pilate conducted many illegal procedures. However, as believers we must remember that the loving Father was in charge at all times through all the darkness. In our most difficult hours, we must throw ourselves on the Father's care as Jesus did.

As the passage opens Jesus and the eleven walk through the eastern gate (now called St. Stephen's) down the hill, across the Kidron Valley to Gethsemane. Our study begins in misery (v. 37) and ends in misery as Peter "went outside and wept bitterly" (v. 75). Though we will find little cheer in these 40 verses, they provide a prelude of the message of the Cross by which our salvation is obtained.

A. PRIVATE MISERY (*Matt. 26:36-46*). The story of Gethsemane is a story of sorrow and failure. Sorrow belongs to the Lord; the failure belongs to the disciples. When we compare Matthew's description with that of Mark and Luke, we learn that Jesus experienced agony of soul such as the disciples had never seen in Him before. Jesus slowly moved from the cheering crowds of the previous Sunday to the overwhelming loneliness of the Cross.

Explaining the Text	*Examining the Text*
1. The word *Gethsemane* means "oil press." It was probably an enclosed garden or orchard which contained some kind of a press used to crush the oil from olives.	1. Read Matthew 26:36-46. Study a map of Jerusalem, tracing the movement of Jesus and the disciples from the city to Gethsemane.
2. The word *sorrowful* means to be grieved or sad to the point of distress (v. 37).	2. What was the "cup" about which Jesus prayed to His Father?
3. The disciples' relaxed behavior stands in stark contrast to the agony and exhaustion of the Lord. (See Luke 22:43-44.)	3. Why did the disciples fall asleep each time Jesus left them? Why did their behavior seem to upset Him so much?
	4. Since Jesus already knew the Father's will, why did He pray that the cup would be taken away?

B. PERVERSE MISERY (*Matt. 26:47-56*). Only John recorded the conversation between Jesus and the crowd that came out to arrest Him, but Matthew gives us the intimate yet tragic dialogue with Judas. Peter found an unexpected courage at the moment of crisis, but he was told by Jesus that, disastrous as the situation appeared to be, all the events were carrying out the will of the Father. The last sentence of this passage emphasizes the failure of the disciples and the aloneness of the Saviour.

Examining the Text	*Explaining the Text*
1. Read Matthew 26:47-56. Why did Jesus still refer to Judas as "friend"? (v. 50)	1. The word for *friend* is *hetaire* meaning "companion" or "associate." It is used only three times in the New Testament, each time by Matthew (20:13; 22:12; 26:50).
2. Study again the description of the crowd that came to arrest Jesus. What kind of rabbi were they expecting to find?	2. Only John named Peter as the disciple with the sword (John 18:10). By the time John's Gospel was circulated, Peter was already dead. Mentioning his name at that time would no longer endanger him with the Roman authorities.
3. Jesus apparently surprised everyone by His responses to the crowd, to the attempt of the disciple to protect Him, and to the servant of the high priest. Why didn't Jesus respond to these situations by calling those "twelve legions of angels"? (v. 53)	3. A Roman legion numbered about 6,000 soldiers. Jesus referred to approximately 72,000 angels, quite enough to protect Him from the armed crowd at Gethsemane.
4. Reread Matthew 26:47-56. Write down how you feel toward:	
Jesus	

Explaining the Text	*Examining the Text*
	the crowd
	Judas
	the chief priests and elders
	the disciples

C. PUBLIC MINISTRY (*Matt. 26:57-68*). This third section of Matthew 26 describes the trial of Jesus before Caiaphas and the Sanhedrin. Review the chart on page 66 and note that there were six trials in all, three religious and three civil. Though Caiaphas tried to find some kind of legal basis to condemn Jesus to death, the whole procedure was in fact illegal.

Explaining the Text	*Examining the Text*
1. Caiaphas, the son-in-law of Annas, was a Sadducee appointed high priest in A.D. 18 by Valerius Gratus. He held that office for 18 years until deposed by Procurator Vitellius in A.D. 36.	1. Read Matthew 26:57-68. Then study John 18:12-14, 19-23. Why did John report that Jesus was first taken before Annas while Matthew says Jesus was taken to Caiaphas?
	2. Use a Bible dictionary or encyclopedia to define *Sanhedrin*. Who made up the ranks of this group? Why was Jesus taken before the Sanhedrin?
	3. Define *blasphemy*. Why did the Sanhedrin think Jesus was guilty of blasphemy?

Examining the Text	Explaining the Text
4. Why did Jesus not answer the question about destroying and rebuilding the temple after He had willingly answered the question about being the Christ, even adding information about the Second Coming?	

D. PERSONAL MISERY (*Matt. 26:69-75*). During Jesus' trial, Peter was tested. Three times he had opportunity to speak up for the Lord; three times he denied he ever knew the prisoner from Gethsemane. He went as far as to call down curses on himself as a way of affirming his innocence. Then the Lord's prophecy was fulfilled; the rooster crowed, and Peter finally grasped what he had done.

Examining the Text	Explaining the Text
1. Read Matthew 26:69-75. When we look at various Gospel accounts to determine the chronology of events, it is called studying a *harmony* of the Gospels. Peter's denial is recorded by all the Gospel writers (Mark 14:66-72; Luke 22:55-62; John 18:17-18, 25-27). Study the other three accounts in conjunction with Matthew's record and list the events in the order you think they occurred.	1. More than likely Peter's three denials did not occur one right after the other but were interrupted over a period of time by other events of the evening recorded in the other Gospels.
2. Name the specific references to Peter's three accusers. On what basis were they claiming that he must have known Jesus? What clues do we have that Peter did or did not understand the Resurrection?	2. Calling curses on oneself is like saying, "May God strike me dead if what I say is not true." If the disaster does not immediately follow, presumably the speaker is innocent.

Explaining the Text	Examining the Text
3. Luke tells us that Jesus looked directly at Peter (Luke 22:61). It may have been that look that finally brought Peter to tears by causing him to remember what Jesus had said earlier.	3. Do you think Peter's tears were tears of genuine repentance? What would lead you to that conclusion? 4. Why did Peter continue to stay in the courtyard while so strongly denying his association with Jesus? 5. Review verses 69-75. How did Peter allow himself to be trapped in this difficult situation?

Experiencing the Text

1. Have you ever been betrayed by a friend? How did you feel when that happened? How could other friends have helped you during that time of difficulty?

2. About what specific things in your life should you be praying, "Not as I will, but as You will"?

3. Matthew 26:41 is often quoted: "The Spirit is willing, but the body is weak." What areas of your life tend to suffer when your resistance is down?

4. Write down three specific things you learned from Jesus' prayer in the Garden of Gethsemane.

5. Matthew 26:56 reports that the disciples deserted Jesus and fled. Have you ever felt that you deserted Jesus when He needed you?

6. How would you advise a person who comes to you and says, "I am a Christian, but I have failed the Saviour miserably"?

Matthew 27:1-66

Murder of the King

A few years ago, a priest at a North Carolina Catholic Church placed his usual array of Lenten crosses draped all in black for Good Friday out in front of his little church. Soon he received a call from the North Myrtle Beach Chamber of Commerce complaining about the crosses in the churchyard. The caller indicated there would be no problem with crosses inside, but out front where everybody could see them, they were offensive. The Chamber was worried about the retired people ("who might find them depressing") and the tourists ("who come down to get happy and don't want to be reminded about Jesus' death"). In short, crosses on the lawn were bad for business (reported by William Willimon, *Context*, May 15, 1986).

Yes, the cross of Christ is offensive, and that's exactly what Jesus told His disciples it would be. In this study, we move from Judas' betrayal and Peter's denial to Jesus' brutal persecution and murder. Murder? Yes. An illegal execution carried out for political purposes can be called nothing else.

As we noticed in our last study, it is always helpful to see a harmony of events in the Gospels, particularly as we study the Crucifixion account. The chart on the following page shows a complete harmony of Crucifixion events.

HARMONY OF EVENTS AT JESUS' CRUCIFIXION

1. Jesus arrived at Golgotha (Matt. 27:33; Mark 15:22; Luke 23:33; John 19:17).
2. He refused the offer of wine mixed with myrrh (Matt. 27:34; Mark 15:23).
3. He was nailed to the cross between the two thieves (Matt. 27:35-38; Mark 15:24-28; Luke 23:33-38; John 19:18).
4. He gave His first cry from the cross: "Father, forgive them, for they do not know what they are doing" (Luke 23:34).
5. The soldiers took Jesus' garments, leaving Him naked on the cross (Matt. 27:35; Mark 15:24; Luke 23:34; John 19:23).
6. The Jews mocked Jesus (Matt. 27:39-43; Mark 15:29-32; Luke 23:35-37).
7. He conversed with the two thieves (Luke 23:39-43).
8. He gave His second cry from the cross, "I tell you the truth; today you will be with Me in paradise" (Luke 23:43).
9. He spoke the third time, "Woman, here is your son" (John 19:26-27).
10. Darkness came from noon to 3 P.M. (Matt. 27:45; Mark 15:33; Luke 23:44).
11. He gave His fourth cry, "My God, My God, why have You forsaken Me?" (Matt. 27:46-47; Mark 15:34-36)
12. His fifth cry was, "I am thirsty" (John 19:28).
13. He drank "wine vinegar" (John 19:29).
14. His sixth cry was, "It is finished" (John 19:30).
15. He drank wine vinegar from a sponge (Matt. 27:48; Mark 15:36).
16. He cried a seventh time, "Father, into Your hands I commit My spirit" (Luke 23:46).
17. He dismissed His spirit by an act of His own will (Matt. 27:50; Mark 15:37; Luke 23:46; John 19:30).
18. The temple curtain was torn in two (Matt. 27:51; Mark 15:38; Luke 23:45).
19. Roman soldiers admitted, "Surely He was the Son of God" (Matt. 27:54; Mark 15:39).

A. BETRAYER OF THE SAVIOUR (*Matt. 27:1-10*). Possibly Judas never believed that his betrayal would produce the results it did. For whatever reason, he acted irrationally twice more in throwing the money in the temple and committing suicide. Even this tragic end fulfills prophecy (Acts 1:13-20).

Examining the Text	*Explaining the Text*
1. Read Matthew 27:1-10. Check a Bible dictionary or encyclopedia for more information on Pilate. Who was he, and what kind of man was he?	1. The brief trial described in Matthew 27:1 was conducted merely to confirm what had happened earlier and to affirm the death penalty.

Explaining the Text	Examining the Text
2. The reference to the temple in verse 5 is the word *naos*, the holy place itself.	2. Compare Judas' response with Peter's response. How were they alike? How were they different?
	3. Find and read the prophecies mentioned by Matthew (Jer. 19:1, 4, 6, 11; Zech. 11:12-13).
3. The land purchased by the Sanhedrin in Judas' name became known as *Akeldama* in Aramaic (Acts 1:19), the field of blood. Previously it apparently had been a place where potters dug for clay.	4. Why were the chief priests so concerned about how the returned blood money was used?
	5. If Judas had come to you for counseling after he took the money back to the temple, what would you have said to him?

B. TRIAL OF THE SAVIOUR (*Matt. 27:11-26*). Matthew gives a brief summary of the trial before Pilate. Because Matthew's main theme was the kingship of Jesus, this passage focuses on Pilate's question. Matthew wrote as though nothing occurred before that crucial question in verse 11.

Explaining the Text	Examining the Text
1. The Roman Empire was divided into provinces such as Achaia and Syria. Some were ruled by proconsuls, and others by proprietors directly answerable to the Emperor. Lesser provinces were placed under procurators like Pilate.	1. Read Matthew 27:11-26. Why did Jesus not reply to the charges brought against Him? Why did this surprise Pilate?

Examining the Text

2. What does the text tell us about Pilate's motive in offering the crowd a choice of Barabbas or Jesus?

3. After proclaiming His innocence publicly, why did Pilate have Jesus flogged as well as crucified?

4. What makes you think Pilate did or didn't heed his wife's warning?

5. If you had been given the opportunity to argue with Pilate regarding his decision, how would you have tried to convince him to let Jesus go free?

Explaining the Text

2. The choice offered by Pilate presents an interesting play on words in the text. Barabbas means "son of the father." The Roman procurator released the false son of the father and executed the true Son of the Heavenly Father.

3. The Greek text shows that the crowd screamed one word—"crucify" (*staurothetō*).

C. SUFFERING OF THE SAVIOUR (*Matt. 27:27-44*). The cross provides the foundation for our salvation—Jesus *died* for our sin. But on the way to the cross He experienced distressing sorrow and suffering. Small wonder we love to sing the hymn that begins, "Man of sorrows."

Explaining the Text

1. The praetorium may have been at Pilate's or Herod's palace. The area must have been quite large, for 600 soldiers (a company or cohort was one tenth of a legion) were present.

2. Simon, who carried the cross, was from Cyrene, a town in what is now known as Libya. Doubtless he had come to Jerusalem for the Passover.

3. The irony of this tragic scene is that Jesus could certainly have done anything the crowd shouted at Him to do. But because of His love for you and me, He renounced all self-preservation and died on that cruel cross.

Examining the Text

1. Read Matthew 27:27-44. In view of Matthew's purpose, what is the significance of the detail he provided in verses 27-31?

2. Why did the Roman soldiers offer Jesus wine to drink? Why did Jesus refuse it?

3. Matthew records that three groups of people "hurled insults" at Jesus while He was dying on the cross. Identify each group and what they said.

4. Reread the description of the Crucifixion. How do you feel toward the Roman soldiers and those who were insulting Jesus? Is there any indication how Jesus felt toward them?

D. DEATH OF THE SAVIOUR (*Matt. 27:45-66*). The awful record of how
God was treated on earth continues in this final section of Matthew 27.
Matthew describes the time, the atmosphere, and the amazing record of the
Resurrection. The segment ends with a common scene in the Gospels, the
faithful following of godly women.

Examining the Text

Explaining the Text

1. Read Matthew 27:45-66. What is the meaning of the
phrase, "He gave up His spirit"? (v. 50)

1. The Aramaic words in
verse 46 represent a quota-
tion of Psalm 22:1. In
Greek the word *eloi* sounds
a bit like Elijah which
may have been why the
crowd thought He was
calling for the ancient
prophet.

2. According to the text, what convinced the cen-
turion that Jesus was the Son of God?

2. The resurrection of
people who came out of
tombs offers a fascinat-
ing story in Matthew's
record. John Walvoord
suggests this was "a fulfillment of the Feast of the
Firstfruits of Harvest men-
tioned in Leviticus
23:10-14. . . . The resurrection of these saints . . .
is a token of the coming
harvest when all the saints
will be raised" (*Matthew:
Thy Kingdom Come*, p.
236).

3. Take a look at John 19:39. Who assisted Joseph in
the burial of Jesus? Why would these two persons be
linked in such a task?

3. The Roman guard
probably sealed the tomb
with the official seal of
cord and wax; the authority
of the Empire was in-
voked to keep the Saviour
in the tomb.

Explaining the Text	*Examining the Text*
	4. Why did the curtain in the temple tear in two from top to bottom? Read Hebrews 10:19-22 for further clarification.

Experiencing the Text

1. Have you ever been unwilling or unable to make a difficult decision? What resources does a Christian have in such situations which were unavailable to Pilate?

2. What are the implications of the dream reported by Pilate's wife? Do you think God speaks in dreams today? Has God ever spoken to you in a dream?

3. Have you ever been caught up in the enthusiasm of a crowd intent on good purposes or bad? What kinds of things happen to make a group of otherwise reasonable people turn into a raving mob like these people at the Crucifixion?

4. Imagine you are standing at the foot of the cross hearing insults poured on Jesus. As you raise your voice above the rest, what do you say to Him?

5. You weren't at the Crucifixion, but Jesus still hears you now. Write a brief paragraph telling Him how you feel about the Crucifixion and its effect on you.

6. Until this time of burial, Joseph of Arimathea was a secret believer. Now he risked his reputation and perhaps more by going public. How have you represented Jesus or shown your love for Him publicly? In what ways might you still do it yet this week?

Matthew 28:1-20

Mastery of the King

Some years ago in the city of Hanover, Germany, a dying infidel left these final instructions for his burial: "When I die, you are to bury my body in an iron vault covered with giant slabs of granite, bound together with iron bands." Finally he insisted, "My tomb is to be sealed with a two-ton block of stone, inscribed with these words: This grave is purchased for eternity. It shall never be opened." And so it was, just as the man had wished. Somehow, though quite mysteriously, a small delicate poplar seed was also buried in that concrete tomb. And then one day, God, in His remarkable wisdom and power, decided it should grow. The tiny stubborn sprout, now surging with new life, forced its way into a tiny crack until one by one, the great iron bands were broken and each giant stone pushed away. Today rising proudly from the center of that open grave is a giant poplar tree, strong testimony to the creative and recreative work of God ("Resurrection Day" by Don Wyrtzen and Phil and Lynne Brower, Singspiration Music, Zondervan).

As we've noticed several times, especially in the last few studies, the order of events during the final weeks of Jesus' life is important but difficult to ascertain. Refer to the chart on the following page for chronological information on the 40 days after Christ's resurrection.

FORTY DAYS—from Resurrection to Ascension

SUNDAY MORNING

1. An angel rolled away the stone from Jesus' tomb before sunrise (Matt. 28:2-4).
2. Women who followed Jesus visited Jesus' tomb and discovered Him missing (Matt. 28:1; Mark 16:1-4; Luke 24:1-3; John 20:1).
3. Mary Magdalene left to tell Peter and John (John 20:1-2).
4. The other women, remaining at the tomb, saw two angels who told them about the Resurrection (Matt. 28:5-7; Mark 16:5-7; Luke 24:4-8).
5. Peter and John visited Jesus' tomb (Luke 24:12; John 20:3-10).
6. Mary Magdalene returned to the tomb and Jesus appeared to her alone in the garden (Mark 16:9-11; John 20:11-18): *His first appearance.*
7. Jesus appeared to the other women (Mary, mother of James, Salome, and Joanna) (Matt. 28:8-10): *His second appearance.*
8. Those who guarded Jesus' tomb reported to the religious rulers how the angel rolled away the stone. They were then bribed (Matt. 28:11-15).
9. Jesus appeared to Peter (1 Cor. 15:5): *His third appearance.*

SUNDAY AFTERNOON

10. Jesus appeared to two men on the road to Emmaus (Mark 16:12-13; Luke 24:13-32): *His fourth appearance.*

SUNDAY EVENING

11. The two disciples from Emmaus told others they saw Jesus (Luke 24:33-35).
12. Jesus appeared to 10 apostles, with Thomas absent, in the Upper Room (Luke 24:36-43; John 20:19-25): *His fifth appearance.*

THE FOLLOWING SUNDAY

13. Jesus appeared to the 11 Apostles, including Thomas, and Thomas believed (John 20:26-28): *His sixth appearance.*

THE FOLLOWING 32 DAYS

14. Jesus appeared to seven disciples by the Sea of Galilee and performed a miracle of fish (John 21:1-14): *His seventh appearance.*
15. Jesus appeared to 500 (including the Eleven) at a mountain in Galilee (Matt. 28:16-20; Mark 16:15-18; 1 Cor. 15:6): *His eighth appearance.*
16. Jesus appeared to His half-brother James (1 Cor. 15:7): *His ninth appearance.*
17. At Jerusalem Jesus appeared again to His disciples (Luke 24:44-49; Acts 1:3-8): *His 10th appearance.*
18. On the Mount of Olives Jesus ascended into heaven while the disciples watched (Mark 16:19-20; Luke 24:50-53; Acts 1:9-12).

A. MASTERY OVER DEATH (*Matt. 28:1-10*). Even the most cursory study of the Book of Acts makes us immediately aware that the Resurrection stands as a foundation for the message of the Gospel. The central theme in apostolic preaching—the fact of Jesus' resurrection—is attested historically in the Gospels and in our study of Matthew, right here in these 10 verses. The day of worship changed from Saturday to Sunday as the Lord broke the bonds of death "at dawn on the first day of the week" (v. 1).

Explaining the Text	*Examining the Text*
1. It will be helpful to study this passage in conjunction with Luke 24:1-8 which provides more details on the message of the angel and the activity of the women.	1. Read Matthew 28:1-10. List several evidences of the Resurrection found in these verses.
2. A harmony of the Gospels suggests that the two women remained at the tomb while Mary Magdalene left to tell Peter and John. See the chart on page 88. Jesus' actual first appearance, therefore, was to Mary Magdalene as she returned the second time to the garden.	2. Name several other historic events in Scripture where God used angels as messengers.
3. Jesus' message to His disciples called them to meet Him in Galilee. We would expect this from Matthew since he made the Galilean ministry a prominent part of his Gospel. Remember also that the disciples were from Galilee and would naturally be returning there after Passover.	3. What reasons might God have had for allowing His risen Son to appear first to women?

Examining the Text	Explaining the Text
4. In a brief paragraph, describe how you would have felt if you had been one of the two Marys on Resurrection morning.	

B. MASTERY OVER EVENTS (*Matt. 28:11-15*). Only Matthew recorded this report of the guards. The whole procedure after the Resurrection reminds us of the trial—falsified, illegal, and self-serving on the part of the Sanhedrin. How interesting that the Jewish religious leaders heard the report of the Resurrection even before the disciples.

Examining the Text	Explaining the Text
1. Read Matthew 28:11-15. Examine the story the guards were told to report. In what ways was it obviously false and even ludicrous?	1. Under Roman law a soldier who fell asleep at his post could be put to death (Acts 12:19).
2. Why did the Roman guards report to the Jewish priests rather than to their military officers?	2. As many have repeatedly pointed out, the body of Jesus was not removed from the tomb by human hands because His friends *could* not do it and His enemies *would* not.
3. Verse 15 says the falsified story was widely circulated right up to the time Matthew wrote his Gospel. Why would people be willing to believe such a fabricated account?	

Explaining the Text	Examining the Text
	4. Why did the chief priests have enough clout with the governor to assure the guards that they would be able to keep them out of trouble? (v. 14)

C. MASTERY OVER HIS DISCIPLES (*Matt. 28:16-20*). The last portion of Matthew 28 records the Galilee meeting prophesied in verses 7 and 10. Once again, Matthew stands alone in recording this significant event which we have come to call the "Great Commission." Some have suggested there may have been a larger crowd even than the 11, but the text doesn't seem to support that notion.

Explaining the Text	Examining the Text
	1. Read Matthew 28:16-20. Notice in verse 17 that "some doubted." What do you think they questioned?
2. Verses 19-20 have been interpreted as a missionary commission, sometimes even to the exclusion of the local church. But the Lord was preparing the disciples to lead the early church as described in Acts 2.	2. Examine all the verbs in verses 19 and 20. Write a paragraph describing what they tell you about the ministry of the church.

Examining the Text

3. How important is baptizing in fulfilling the Great Commission? State your views on when and how people should be baptized.

Explaining the Text

3. The last word of the Gospel of Matthew is the Greek word *aionos* which is translated as "age." Certainly it is true that Jesus goes with us anywhere in the world, but this passage focuses on time. The Lord of the church will be with His church until time ends.

4. Why is it important to know that Jesus will be with His people till the end of the age?

Experiencing the Text

1. How would you defend or "prove" the Resurrection to an unbeliever?

2. How would you respond to the argument that the disciples stole Jesus' body?

3. If you are a Christian, one could say you live in "Resurrection life." What does that mean, and how does it affect your day-by-day lifestyle?

4. This passage tells us that the 11 disciples worshiped Jesus (v. 17). In what specific ways do you worship Jesus other than in church?

5. How are you fulfilling the Great Commission in your life at the present time?

6. Write at least five new things this study of the second half of Matthew has taught you about Jesus.